For Lois

For Jill

with warmest
best wishes,
and gratitude.

[signature]

MR. BRISTOL'S BARN

With Excerpts from Mr. Blinn's Diary

Edited and with photographs by

JOHN SZARKOWSKI

HARRY N. ABRAMS, INC., PUBLISHERS

Editor: James Leggio
Designer: Dirk Luykx

Library of Congress Cataloging-in-Publication Data

Szarkowski, John.
Mr. Bristol's barn: with excerpts from Mr. Blinn's diary / John Szarkowski
p. cm.
ISBN 0–8109–4286–0 (clothbound)
1. Architectural photography—New York (State)—Canaan.   2. Barns—New York
(State)—Canaan—Pictorial works.   3. Traditional farming—New York (State)—Canaan—
History—19th century.   4. Blinn, Philo—Diaries.   I. Blinn, Philo   II. Title
TR659.S93   1997
779' .4'092—dc20   96-27198

Excerpts from the diary of Philo Blinn courtesy of George Dardess and John Dardess

Published in 1997 by Harry N. Abrams, Incorporated, New York
A Times Mirror Company

Printed and bound in Japan

Contents

Mr. Bristol's Barn

I live on a former farm. When the meadow is freshly cut, some passersby might think it a farm still, but they would be mistaken, for no farming is done here. The fact saves me an enormous burden of hard work and deep worry, but it does exact a price in guilt. What the town counts as my and my wife's fields were cleared by others; our views were won by their work. Other men cut and hauled and hewed the timbers that support what is now (for a while) our barn, and with their oxen or horses and stoneboats they muscled into place the great boulders on which they and their neighbors somehow raised walls that rested on level sills.

Our former farm is smaller, considered as a farm, than the one that lay on the same ground earlier. In this country one cannot walk far, at right angles to the town road and into middle-aged woods, without coming to a stone wall—not a well-laid wall of fractured slate, of the sort one admires in (for example) eastern Connecticut—but slumping linear piles, triangular in section, of melon-shaped field-stones. It is hard to believe that these fences, even when new, ever kept an animal in or out, even a sheep, and doubtless they were not intended to. They were intended to clear parcels of ground for agriculture. When no more stones could be piled on top of the fences, great cones of them were piled in the fields. One finds these cones now occasionally in the woods, monuments to the god of work, lost from view after their makers, or their children, gave up and moved to Ohio, where there was more dirt between the stones. After that the trees advanced again into the fields, fields that were scarcely older than the oldest citizen.

It may be that these hill farms were never quite sustainable, except by secret infusions of money from back home, or from a job in the village; or perhaps they were sustained for a while by drawing on the accumulated capital of muscle and body fat and alertness that had been earned in some earlier venue. Or perhaps some of them were marginally viable, until they were brought down by the railroads; or by McCormick's reaper, which gave an advantage to the farmer of flatter land; or by improved roads, which facilitated the escape of wives and children to the towns. In any case, and for whatever reasons, the decline of farms like mine began early. From the evidence of the stone fences that run through our woods, I would guess that the open land on our farm was shrinking by the turn of the century.

It seems clear that our farm produced no cash crop worthy of the name. Judging from the barn, the traction was supplied by a single team of horses, the most recent, whose names are still recorded above the gates of their stalls, were mares named Minnie and Bess. Twenty-five years ago I asked my father, then in his eighties, how many acres might be required to supply the food energy required by one team of draft horses. How many acres, in other words, need one clear and clean and plow and harrow and rake and fertilize and seed and cultivate and reap and shock and thresh to supply the equivalent of what is now gas for a fairly small tractor. After rather complicated excuses involving the unreliability of his memory, my father guessed that sixteen acres might be about right. Pleased with the precision of his guess, I neglected to ask him whether that included only oats and hay, or pasture also.

Whatever his answer might have been, it is clear, in a larger sense, that supporting Minnie and Bess was too much work, and that once it became possible to replace them with a steel tractor—which one could curse without regret, and which ate only fossil fuel that was delivered to the door in a truck—only a saint or other fanatic would continue to work hard enough to make horses work even harder. When the oil is gone, and if we have not learned to do it with solar collectors or windmills, or tiny and powerful nuclear batteries encased in lead capsules no bigger than thimbles, we will perhaps look again with practical interest at the thicker-legged, broader-chested, serious-minded horses, such as the Belgian, the Shire, the Percheron, and the Clydesdale. But until and unless that necessity greets us, it would be merely sentimental to mourn the passing of Minnie and Bess, especially for those of us who never rose in the dark to feed, harness, and tell lies to our horses, even before doing the same for ourselves.

In its best years my former farm might have been hard-pressed to show one hundred dollars of cash income per annum, and producing even that required people to work harder than we now think people should. Hard labor is ennobling up to a point that has not been precisely located, after which it is merely exhausting. Thoreau was a clear observer, and he said:

> How many a poor immortal soul have I seen well-nigh crushed and smothered under its load, creeping down the road of life, pushing before it a barn seventy-five feet by forty, its Augean stables never cleansed, and one hundred acres of land, tillage, mowing, pasture, and wood-lot! The better part of the man is soon plowed into the soil for compost.
> The mass of men lead lives of quiet desperation.

And yet, we do not altogether believe Thoreau, in spite of the excellence of his prose. We would believe him absolutely, except for the contrary evidence provided by certain surviving works of the men he speaks of. Of these surviving works the most impressive are perhaps their barns, which do not seem the work of desperate men.

The ordinary timber barn, such as the one seen here, is an object of high quality, and the expression of an ancient technology that was still evolving well into the nineteenth century. It was in general better made and more cleverly designed than the house nearby, since it required larger rooms and longer spans between columns, which were asked to support greater weights. And it represented in some ways the center of the enterprise.

The timber barn was replaced by the balloon-frame barn before the nineteenth century was over, and the new system was a typical American improvement: it was cheaper, faster, and easier to build, and it was made of standardized, mass-produced parts—dimension material from the sawmill and machine-made nails—from which any reasonably competent person could build a barn from a simple drawing. The frame of a timber barn, in contrast, was made from the trunks of trees, fashioned to a degree of regularity with ax and adze and two-handled drawknife, and fastened together by mortise and tenon and wooden pegs. There were no standardized parts, and every joint was a special case. The buildings were expensive in terms of the material they used, the time they took to build, and the cost of the skilled mechanics who tailored them, but this was not understood until something cheaper was available.

As early as 1854, Mr. Solon Robinson reported to the American Institute of the City of New York on the method and great advantages of the balloon frame, which was already being used in California and Chicago and elsewhere in the experimental West. Mr. Youmans of Saratoga County, New York, had also been impressed by the new system, but added that on his farm he had great difficulty getting the carpenters to try it. "They could not give up tenons and mortises, braces and big timbers, for the light ribs, two by four inches, of a balloon frame." Dr. Church had also seen balloon-frame buildings in the West; he reported that they looked good and strong, but he doubted their durability. Mr. Robinson responded that he was a Christian, and as such was instructed "to take no thought for the morrow"[*] (presumed laughter).

Dr. Church was right in thinking the timber frame durable, as long as the roof stays tight against the weather and the foundation reasonably level. Many, like ours, have survived beyond their own culture, and stand now serving no function worthy of their quality, except as monuments to the ambitions of the farmers who built them, and as unwanted moral dilemmas to their current owners. (A responsible parent must, of course, educate the children before leveling the barn. And yet, some people have done brilliantly without formal education, and the barn will clearly fail soon without attention.)

In fact, there are still many good timber barns in eastern America, doubtless many better than mine (although none more beautifully sited), and it would be a mistake, I think, to make them the spotted owls of vernacular architecture. Nevertheless, they are all different; each one was made by hand according to principles that prevailed before Eli Whitney invented the idea of interchangeable parts. And each one is a record of its own history of use and revision. (Even the milk cows—a succession of them—wore smooth with their necks the rough lumber of their stanchion.) And each one is the instrument of a one-way communication—from the dead to the living: a family of sorts, related not by blood or belief, but by the shared knowledge of a place.

J. S.

[*]"Balloon Frames of Farm Buildings," *Transactions of the American Institute of the City of New York for the Year 1854* (Albany: C. Van Bentheusen, 1855), pp. 398–99.

Mr. Blinn's Diary

January 22, 1859:   *This evening Mr. Geo. F. Morgan called here to sell me a horse. I did not want it, but he insisted so strongly that I bo't it. I had an old note against him of 9$, and he had a note against me to partially offset. I gave him his old note, 20$ in money, and my note (6 mo.) for 10$ amounting probably in all to about 35$. Then I saddled wife's mare "Beauty", and rode over to John Wagner's and sold him the old mare I had of J. Gardner Hollenbeck for 14 sheep. Then on to Ezra Cady's, paid him 129$ due on his sheep. On the way I saw Dr. Willcox, and paid him 20$ and turned in a bill for lumber $12.50, making in all $32.56. Came round by the store home in a stiff north west breeze and a snow squall. When I got in by the fire found I was used up; had pleurisy pain in left side, and out of sorts generally. Bridget* gone home, Henry† a-bed, babies asleep, and wife and I alone. No one to interfere in our review of the week that's past. It has gone as very many has gone before it, busy in buying, selling, trading and getting gain for this life without I fear any advance in Spiritual gain. It is strange, when I am warned so often of my weakness, my frailty, that I am not admonished.*

---

*Bridget Daile was the Blinn's hired girl, who normally went home to her own family at the end of the day.

†Henry Gott, the hired man, lived with the Blinns.

February 6, 1859:   *We have had the "blues" and want to sell out, for the labor is too much where there is so much to do as there is here. There is no shirking it. We have all to put our shoulder to the wheel. We went to Church this A.M., but we are so out of sorts that we could not go to the monthly concert; it is held this evening at the Center Schoolhouse.*

February 7, 1859:   *We are better, thanks to him who dispenses blessings.*

14

February 13, 1859: *Attended Church this A.M. . . . The sermon contrasted the difference in conditions now, and after death. Now we have everything to hope for, life eternal is freely offered, yes, urged upon us; we have but to believe and exercise faith and it is ours; but after death there is a deep impassable gulph between the State of blessedness, and misery; then change, or hope, or expectation of a change is not. Just at night Mr. Square's man came here with 4 fat cattle to stay the night; put the cattle up; and got the supper going for him & wife and I went up to the schoolhouse for meeting.*

March 2, 1859: *I have been very idle today. I think I am becoming positively lazy, but there are good reasons why I should not over exert myself. My health is very much better when I am quiet, and if I could sell this great cumbersome grain farm, I would try and divest myself of all cares that require such bodily exertion.*

May 27, 1859:   *Our cattle and sheep came in this morning. . . . Carter‡ put the cattle into his swamp, and I took the sheep on the School house lots. We rec'd letter from Shelden saying that we must go and meet him at once, and receive our drove sheep. Matters are thickening. There is a prospect of a great deal of work, care, & trouble, and I feel again as if I had been very foolish to have anything to do with it, and wish from the bottom of my heart that I could let this droving-speculating business go, and attend to our farming matters & let that suffice.*

June 9, 1859:   *This evening traded with Hollenbeck: let him have a little dwarf colt we had of Jacob Ceaser, 7 yards satinett, and are to pay him 45$ in money, for five sheep and five lambs and one fat cow. Cow and colt exchanged, cloth delivered, the sheep and lambs to run in his pasture until September. Mr. Phelps from Otis, Mass. with us over night, on his way to Albany to meet a drove [of] cattle.*

June 10, 1859:   *We commenced planting our corn over this morning—the worms are doing great injury to it. About 11 o'clock it commenced to rain, and broke off for the day. Now one of the sheep drivers came home again today—we have them both here all the time—they have not stopped at Carter's at all. Bridget went home this P.M.; Wife doing the work alone, taking care of 5 men, 2 babies, and 5 cows.*

June 12, 1859:   *This morning we found a killing frost on the ground. Corn, punkins & 11 kinds of garden vines, potatoes, were cut down to the ground.*

‡Aaron Carter Blinn was Philo's brother and his partner in various trading ventures.

June 15, 1859:   *Sheared 185 sheep today. Carter went over &*
rec'd 15 sheep we contracted of J.A. Blinn some time ago at 4$
each, wool off. They will probably lose 50¢ each. We are making
no sales, and the prospects look decidedly bad. We shall probably
lose money on the whole investment, besides our time & the use of
all, or nearly all, our pasture. But I have one consoling thing about
it, that is, this is my last drove, make or lose it. Am bound not to
make a slave of myself any longer. We—wife and I—are completely
worn out with cares attending this droving business. I have grown
prematurely old in the business. I may have more dollars in the
trade; I am sure I have more sins by it, for it's a hard traffic for the
conscience.

June 17, 1859:   *We have got off 183 sheep today—6 shearers;*
one is a boy, and one no better than a boy. It has rained most of this
P.M. We have about 90 sheep shut up that will do tomorrow.
Then we shall have to lay over until next week. Sold three today to
G. W. Lovejoy for 4¢ per lb; weighed 124 lb., yearlings.

June 19, 1859:   *Attended Church with Wife at the School house*
this A.M. This Afternoon we took John to the same place. He
behaved quite well. Mr. Blain's afternoon discourse was a very
searching one, and I am very sorry there were so few to hear it. His
text was in the Prophesy of Hosea, 11:8 & 9. Mr. Blain preaches
such plain, practical, convincing touches, and in such a meek and
feeling manner, that they cannot fail to do very much good. He is, I
think, emphatically a good man.

24

July 1, 1859:   Wife, Caroline & I went up to the church to select seats. They were all taken but 7, those not the most desirable ones. Still, they are good enough.

July 2, 1859:   This P.M. it has been quite warm & toward night there was quite an extensive prospect of thunder showers. The whole western, southern, and northern horizon was one dense black cloud. It began to rain while we were taking tea. It was not very powerful at first, but soon after it, the first shower, and before it had quite done raining, the clouds gathered over us, and we were completely deluged, our meadows all swept over, the fence taken off, the whole surface from here to Mr. Hollenbeck's covered with water. I dammed up above Mr. Willcox's barn, and we thought it would carry it off, and I think it would, had we not opened the fence & given the water free course. It has been and is the wildest storm, the greatest rain I ever witnessed. It is still raining very fast, 11 o'clock. Mr. Wilcox hired woman & a little boy are here for safe keeping. Mrs. Wilcox not at home, Mr. Wilcox watching to see his house go off. How much we are damaged, we cannot tell, but we know it must be very heavy. Our grass is ruined, all or nearly all of it. Rec'd of D.W. Curtis 83$, ballance due on note. Pd 30$ of it to wife. She claimed more.

July 3, 1859:   *This morning revealed to us the devastations of last night's flood. For it truly was a flood. Our meadows washed nearly all over & the water still running down thru them from the road, & all the lower part one unbroken sheet of water. Our fences along the road taken down and taken off; the sod of our corn lot, the Pierson Orchard washed into the street. . . . But our damage is slight in comparison to some of our neighbors. Mr. Wilcox has an acre of ground part of it covered 2 to 4 feet deep with stones & gravel, other parts of it the soil all washed out in deep gullies. Mr. Fowler's buildings were nearly undermined. S.D. Ford's barns, the underground part filled with gravel and stone. The flood came down with so much force it broke in on the upper side of his shed or hog house, broke every board and most of the timbers. The sluice above Fowler's gone, and the earth and stone where it stood. The sluice above S.D. Ford by the lane to the quarry washed away, and the earth washed out 10 feet deep & 20 wide. Mr. Lape's mill dam swept away—in fact, all have suffered more or less. But I am thankful to be able to record that there were no lives lost, no bodily injury as far as heard from. Today our Church was opened. It's finished beautifully, so neat and plain. I like it very much & think the whole Society are well pleased. Rev. Theo. Brown preached the dedicatory sermon today to a full house, notwithstanding the last night's freshet & the broken roads. It was a fine discourse, and wonderfully and very appropriate. His text 2:9 Haggai: "The Glory of this latter house shall be greater than that of the former, saith the Lord of Hosts".*

July 4, 1859: *I have been thinking to the many 4th of July Celebrations I have attended, but I do not remember of ever spending one that in retrospect was so blessed as the past—this one that we have been and are enjoying now. To enumerate all the blessings and pleasures of the past day would be an endless task; but some of the more prominent I must mention. (1st), we have been blessed with and enjoyed health, (2nd) our family relations are all truly pleasant, (3rd), we are in the undisputed enjoyment of enough of the things of this world to supply all our earthly wants, (4) we hope and believe we are in possession of better views of ourselves & our felloe men & our God than we ever were before, and, (5th) we sold our wool—1700 fleeces—for 45¢ per lb.; and I have been having considerable anxiety about that. This afternoon by invitation Wife and I attended a party at D.D. Warner's. It was extremely pleasant, and a great many there, all in full enjoyment. Truly, I feel life is worth living for.*

July 10, 1859: *Attended Church this A.M. with John. He behaved very well. I was so tired that I could not enjoy the exercises at all. I hope the time shall soon come that I shall not be obliged to work so hard through the week, that I cannot keep awake through a short discourse.*

July 24, 1859: *We attended Church this A.M. We had a sermon from the 15th Chapter of 1st Corinthians, on the resurrection of the body. To some it may appear clear, but to me it does not. The Spiritual resurrection seems plain. I had a long <u>swoon</u> this afternoon of 2½ hours; feel quite refreshed. Wife paid 3$ today to Miss Sarah Warner for Church repairs—making in all that we have paid for the improvement of the Church 38$, and we feel that our money is well invested.*

July 31, 1859: *I fear I grow worse and more worldly, instead of better and more spiritual. I staid from Church all day today. Bridget went to Chatham, so wife could not go. I was tired and excused myself. Mr. Blain exchanged with Rev. Mr. Decker of New Concord today & I would have liked much to hear him.*

August 18, 1859:   *Today we all—Martha Goodrich, Carter's girls, Wife and I in our carriage, Carter & wife & John in their buggy—went to Campmeeting down near Chatham 4 Cors. There was a great many people there. We staid in the evening. Saw the way they did all through; and we think that Campmeetings are a glorious religious humbug, to most people. Still, there may be a class reached by the loose, rollicking way they preach, sing and pray out in the woods, that would not view any other way. The means of Grace has been blessed in by-gones, and probably will be again. We got home 1/2 past 11 o'clock at night; if not better, we hope wiser than we went.*

September 10, 1859: *Helen is no better. Wholly confined to her bed. Dr. here twice today. Marietta & I went to Puncetta this P.M. Had what is considered to have there a good visit—found them well. William was so much engaged with his cares that he could not come in until just as we started to come away. If he ever comes here I hope we may give him a warm reception & treat them as people should be treated. It rained lightly all the way over and back. Mrs. Fowler came down and attended to Helen's wants while we were gone.*

September 11, 1859: *We felt that Helen was some better this morning, but in the middle of the day she seemed not so well. This evening we feel positive she is better. She thinks she is, too. This is our 4th wedding anniversary—we have not celebrated it only in heartfelt silent thanks to Almighty God that we are still spared to one another; that he has blessed us with two lovely, bright & healthy children; and for, too, those several earthly blessings—we truly have very much to be thankful for.*

September 12, 1859: We called Helen better again this morning, but it's no such thing. I fear she is no better, but that she is worse every day. This afternoon and evening she has been very bad. She cannot bear the least excitement. We can hardly move her from one side of the bed to the other. She is very much reduced. Still, I hope and believe she will rally soon and begin to recover. Marietta is with us. She goes tomorrow. I don't know how we will do when she is gone. I hope she will be rewarded for all her kindness to us.

September 18, 1859: We have had a trying time for & thro the past week. Mrs. Blinn has been very, very sick. She was just on the borders of eternity, to all appearances. But thro the mercys of an all-wise & good God she is spared yet to us. And we think she is getting better as fast as she aught. She is now so she sits up to eat her meals & does pretty good justice to them.

November 12, 1859: We have had so little transpiring with us for the last ten days that I have not written. We have been farming, working very hard, done a great [deal?] of work, and accomplished nothing. We have been ditching and filling the blind with stone. The weather has been beautiful—warm and dry—until yesterday, when the wind changed into the north; blew a gale, & cold. It blew down a shed over at the Pierson's barn; and now we have got to put up another, in the snow, if it comes. We have had Chas. Ingersol here to help us two days, drawing stone for drains. He is very poor, and I feel sorry for the foolish, misguided fellow. He has learned no wisdom from all his misfortunes. He had, I suppose, 3 to 4000$ left him and his wife, and he has let it all slip thro his fingers. And now, all unaccustomed to it, has to out for labor by the day. How closely money should be watched, if we have it entrusted to us! For those that are accustomed to have money, and become poor, make the poorest kind of poor.

November 21, 1859: *This P.M. wife and I attended the funeral of Thos. Bishop in Red Rock. Elder Gallup officiated. Text, Isaiah 61st, 2nd, last clause; "To comfort all that mourn". The effort of the discourse seemed to be, that Christ's mission here in the flesh was to comfort all that were in affliction, & mourn over & for their sins; & that as we live so shall we die; if to the Lord, we die in the Lord; but if in sin, we die in sin, & must suffer its consequences. Leaving the Congregation to draw their own conclusions as to the deceased's life. He done quite as well as he usually does, although it was not a very brilliant discourse. Rec'd for tallow of Mr. Cady $1.10. Pd. 53¢ for goods.*

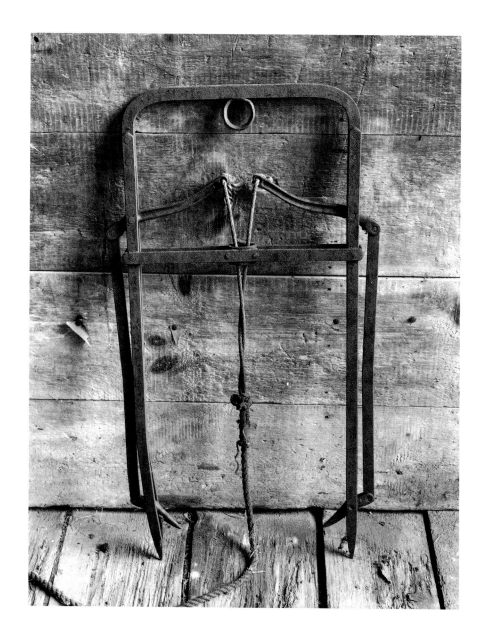

November 24, 1859: *This morning wife got out her old mare, and went over to Mrs. Pratts. Returned in time to take me to church. Mr. Blain gave us the first political discourse he ever preached to us. The pith of it was, That he did not consider there was any or much danger to the welfare of our government from any of the causes agitated by the political parties of the day (meaning slavery); & tacitly admitting the institution a just one. . . . He seemed to think there were numberless sins that were greater than the wholesale system of concubinage in the South, than the custom of fathers selling their own offsprings into perpetual slavery, of the owners selling and breaking up families, parting them asunder, taking the child from the mother, husband from wife, making chattel of God's own image, cramping and distorting the very soul which was given by God to all free and independent. He seemed to think that any expressed desire to better the condition, or free those that are in bonds, is a greater sin than any of the above mentioned. . . . I am glad that I do not think so; and if I did, wish some kind friend would enlighten me. Mr. Blain I believe to be a good Christian.*

December 11, 1859: *Wife, John & I attended Church this A.M. Mr. Blain preached from Revelations, 3rd chap. 20th. verse: "Behold, I stand at the door and knock; if any man hear my voice & open the door I will come in to him and sup with him, & he with Me." It was vain & useless, he said, for anyone to say that Christ had not knocked at the door of their hearts for admission; nevertheless, even with God's express command to do so, not all could open their hearts and receive God, for if they could, the whole world would be saved; and God had ordained that it should not be so. That, he said, was one of the mysteries of Godliness. Had it not been for the incongruity of the last part of the sermon, I think his effort would have been the most successful I ever heard from him; but, that almost spoiled it for me.*

December 13, 1859: . . . *When I got home I found wife so much out of sorts that I sent for Dr. Coffin. He spent the evening visiting with me, & finally put his horse in the stable and concluded to wait to see what the event would be. Nelson worked here today, getting our corn.*

December 14, 1859: *This morning wife about the same. I was up with her pretty much all night. Mrs. Wilcox came 3 o'clock A.M. Staid until daylight. After breakfast the Dr. went home. He returned about noon and went home again. Mrs. Lovejoy came in about 9 o'clock A.M. & has just gone home. Carter's wife here most all day. And about 3 o'clock P.M. there was an advent here. Things came to a crisis. Wife presented us with a weest bit of a little girl that ever was. And now both mother and child seem to be doing well. Dr. Coffin called this evening, but found he was too late, & went directly home again. Dr. Bostwick & sister called here this evening for a visit. I dismissed them sans ceremony. We are all well worn with watching. I attend to the wants of the wee one & her mother tonight.*

December 15, 1859: *The last night passed very comfortable. The little one complained with all the strength and noise she had at her cold treatment, so we wrapped her in hot flannels, and all went to bed. Looking at her out from among the sheets this morning I find her quite a comely featured, plump, & apparently healthy little one. She is tho't to be 2 to 3 months premature. Still, with a strong inclination to try the realities of life, and with close watching and careful nurturing we hope to keep her. Wife quite as comfortable as could be expected, and from present appearances think she will get up as soon as it will be considered advisable.*

December 20, 1859: *Our little babe died last night at about 11 o'clock. She died just as we began to hope and believe she would live. It was to us a most unexpected stroke. We had tho't her healthy, & quite as likely to live as any child. Wife is completely prostrated. I have tried to divert her mind and rally her spirits, all to no avail. We loved the little unexpected gift more than we knew or thought. We had forgotten God gave it, that it was his, and that now he has taken her to himself. May we be reconcilled to his will, and oh! may our wills be reconcilled to him.*

December 26, 1859: *We have had a dark day—just such a day as we poor miserable worldlings need to show us how frail, weak, and dependent we are. A day that we are brought up to a full stop, and left partially on our own resources to see and feel our own unsoundness, spiritually and physically.*

September 9, 1860:   *Wife, children & I attended church today. I have been from home for 2 Sabbaths preceeding this, & I enjoyed the day very much with our family. Mr. Blain was not remarkably luminous; still, I suppose he gave us what would be called by the orthodox a sound, argumentative discourse. His text the 3rd petition in Our Lord's Prayer, vis., "Give us this day our daily bread," drawing conclusions therefrom that we must ask God's blessing, and acknowledging His goodness in the most trivial of our every day occurrences. He made a little desertion from his text, trying to prove, & positively asserting that money or riches was & is a very great curse to its possesser; that the heart grows colder, & the grasp grows tighter with each and every business success; and the wealthier the man, the more naked and the more wicked. I think Mr. Blain's view in some things show a great [lack] of worldly experience.*

September 28, 1860: *. . . This is my 39th birthday. I feel that I am getting to be, almost, an old man, without accomplishing anything worthy of notice.*

Photograph on opposite page:
The inscription on the door to the stables reads: "Minds of all great/men remind us,/and parting leave/behind us footprints/upon the sands/of time. /5,30,92."
    The writer was quoting from memory, and got Longfellow's poem a little wrong. The original says: "Lives of great men all remind us/We can make our lives sublime,/And, departing, leave behind us/Footprints on the sands of time."
    The date "5,30,92" was Decoration Day (Memorial Day), twenty-seven years after the end of the Civil War.

December 23, 1860:   *Wife, John & I attended church this A.M. at the Centre. Mr. Blain was not very fortunate in selecting ideas to expound & elucidate his text, it being the 8th & 9th Commandments. The whole congregation, including most, & I guess all, his church members were dissatisfied with [his] ideas as advanced in reference to stealing. He would cut all mankind off from all kind and manner of deals;—that is, the buyer should at all times pay all an article was worth, & the seller should never ask or take any more. That kind of trade would do away with all business men; in fact, there would be no regular value to anything, for no one would buy only [except] to supply an immediate want. I fear his discourse was not calculated to do much good. We all like Mr. Blain, & think him a very good man, but some of us think his preaching is not doing us any good. Rather a still, cold, unpalatable religion his.*

April 22[?], 1861: Mr. D. L. Ford has been here a great part of the time today, talking of the war news. The times are very exciting—war, and rumors of war—the report tonight is that Baltimore has been burnt by the government troops, and is under martial law. There is a meeting at East Chatham tonight to enlist troops.

July 23, 1861: I mowed in the meadow by Mr. Holenbeck's this morning, & broke the machine again. Had to go to Mr. Bates, to have it mended. This P.M. we drew in five loads. Jake commences cutting the rye. We rec'd today the news of the great defeat of our Federal forces at Manassas Junction, in Virginia—4000 to 5000 killed, & the utter rout of our Army. The news was too much for my weak nerves—I was completely unhinged all the fore part of the day. We had never tho't that _our_ army could meet with such reverses; we had anticipated nothing but success. I really never before _felt_ the horrors of war.

September 28, 1861: *The men threshed rye with flails an hour or two this morning, then went to cutting corn. Messinger laying stone fence. Mr. Russell returned, & took dinner with us. I went to E. Chatham, to mill, this P.M. Took 12 bush. hog feed, 5 bush. rye for flour. Commenced feeding pumpkins to the fat cattle tonight—1 pair oxen, 1 cow. No frost yet, to kill vines. Paid Chas Messinger 5$ on his work. Rec'd. of Ira Smith on account A.C. & P.B. Blinn 100$. This has been my fortyeth birthday. I am getting to be an old man; the retrospect is anything but flattering. . . . I have all the while been so very busy getting ready to live, or in other words, getting something to live on, that I have never thought to improve, to value, to enjoy the present.*

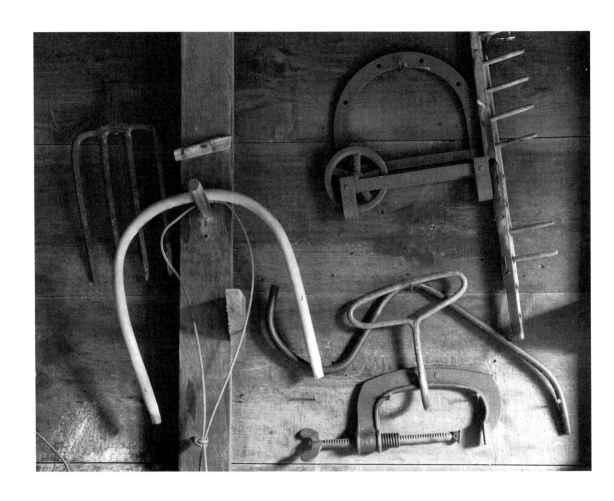

March 22, 1864:   *Wife and Sarah took "Friskey" and drove to Green River. Sarah staid for a visit; wife returned this P.M. I went up to McGovern's and bo't of him a pair of oxen at 140$, a cow and yearling at 42$, a sow pig at 6$; 18 fowls at 8$, lot of old chains at 2$, an old cradle at 2$—in all amounting to 200$. He owed A.C. & P.B. Blinn 40$, which he allowed on the purchase. I paid him 30$ and gave him my note on demand for the ballance, 130$. He delivered the traps and stock. I gave him and his boy a good warm dinner, a pan of meat to take home, and the fellow went off with quite a light heart. Chauncey Lot came & paid the note he gave I.A. Smith of 180$ and interest 19$. Then he bo't a cow of me for 43$ that I bo't of R. Olmsted a week ago today at 35$. I bo't of Dr. Lusk a gobble turkey, gave him 1$ for him, and bro't him home under my arm on horseback.*

March 27, 1864: *Wife and I attended church this A.M. Mr. Elliot preached, or talked to us, about what kind of place he thought Heaven to be. He made it a place full of shady bowers, crystal brooks, moss-covered rocks, flowery dales, forest-chills—in fine, a splendid place for recreation, a fine place for thought, and the prosecution of scientific studies, a splendid place for artists (to sketch and paint the beautiful scenery I suppose), a place occupied by redeemed spirits, little children and angels. But I was curious to know where the Creator is.*

May 21, 1864: *We all attended church today at the Center. The minister, from Lebanon, preached in exchange with Mr. Whiting. He is quite young. He preached well, perhaps a little flowery, but that will wear off with the Spring.*

November 25, 1866:   *Ned, Sarah and I went to Church this A.M. Mr. Boughton preached and gave us a very good sermon, from these words: "If the Lord be God, serve him; but if Baal be God, serve him. How long halt ye between two opinions?" I felt that for me I would not halt any longer, but would at once choose between the two, and declare to the world that as for me and my home we will serve the Lord.*

January 11, 1867:   *Thursday Mr. and Mrs. W. C. Niles, E. S. Barrett, Dr. Coffin and Miss G. were here to dinner. Mr. Barrett and I came to an agreement about trading farms on Thursday. Mr. Barrett takes our land here and at the Centre at 13,800$, I take his at $6000, our writings to be made next Thursday, when we give full deeds and the mortgage is to be made. I sent the money to pay our tax Thursday $48.70. I sold today the land at the Center, to A.S. Bates for 1000$ on Barrett's account.*

January 16, 1867:   *I am nervous and weak tonight—don't know what causes it, unless 'tis that we have tomorrow to deed away our home and nearly all our real estate.*

November 27, 1873:   *We have enjoyed a very pleasant*
Thanksgiving, all at home, and all in good health excepting wife,
and she convalescing slowly, just well enough to enjoy her children
around her—and all at home after their short absence. Sarah is
looking well, feeling finely—and we judge is improving under her
Normal instruction fully as much, if not more, than she would or
could under treatment at a more fashionable and expensive school.
John has not been long enough away to know much about his
school, altho' he likes it well, and we hope he will improve his time
to the best advantage, for this is probably his last time at school; he
being more of a farmer than a scholar. Philo[Jr.] attends school in
our district graded school, with how much profit one can hardly tell.
To say that he does not learn would be telling an untruth; but
whether his learning is most of what is taught at school, or what he
picks up on the streets, is a question.

November 28, 1873:   *We have been very quiet all day. I deliv-*
ered side of beef to B. Niles; thence home, and done choars. This
evening our children have all gone to Spencertown, to a surprise
party to Henry Niles. John took Miss Ida Mull, Sarah went with
Edward Niles, Philo went with Milton Niles.

November 29, 1873:   *Our children returned this morn at 3 o'c.*
E. Niles spent the night, and took breakfast. I went to Geo. Miller's
to look at some sheep this P.M. Otherwise been completely idle. The
weather is fine and sleighing beautiful. Our winter commenced very
early, but if it goes through as finely as it has gone this far, we shall
have no reason to complain if it is long.

December 14, 1873: *John took Nellie to church today, wife and I staid at home. I have spent most of the day reading a Jewish work, "The Women of Israel", and have been both instructed and edified. As years increase, I feel more disinclined to go out. I like the quiet Sabbath Day best, and sometimes feel that I may perhaps fulfill the requirements of the law as well in peaceful, quiet rest at home, with good instructive reading, and the Bible always at hand, as to get out with show and pomp with others to public worship, where the comments are made about this and that one's appearance, how much this one put in the contribution box, and how much that one ought to, and where all who go now, and sit under our present teacher's direction, feel an unsupportable heaviness weighing down their eyelids—or quarrelsome that they are obliged to sit and hear a man talk who has nothing to say.*

About Mr. Bristol and Mr. Blinn

The barn in these photographs was built about the time of the American Civil War, by (or for) Abel Ingersol Bristol. Bristol (1832–1880) was one of three sons of Eliphalet Bristol (1784–1869), and one of many grandchildren of his father's father, also called Eliphalet, who was born in Connecticut a quarter century before the Declaration of Independence, and who at the age of nineteen moved to the frontier—to Canaan, New York—where he bought land from William Warner, one of forty-four (or forty-three) speculators[*] who in 1754 bought thirty-six square miles from the Stockbridge Indians, for two hundred and fifty pounds. It was thought at the time that the area was a part of the Massachusetts Bay Colony, but it proved in time to be part of New York.

The beautiful 1858 E. A. Balch map of Columbia County identifies Abel Bristol as proprietor of the farm in question, but the small square dot that indicates improvements was then at the north end of the meadow, where now only a few boulders mark the foundation of an earlier barn, and much fainter marks indicate what was presumably then the house. Those buildings had (I think) been part of the earlier farm of Nathanial Bacon, which had been bought in part by Abel's father. In the Beers Atlas of 1873 the land is again identified as that of A. Bristol, but a second square dot indicates that new buildings had been built a quarter mile down the hill. It is possible that the migration downstream was an effort to gain better access to water: there are at least four dug wells on the farm, preceding the present drilled well of 1936; the dug wells are now generally dry by August, and it seems likely that even in 1870 they could not be depended on to last until the late September rains.

The name by the square black dot on the map may in fact indicate not the owner but the occupant; Abel Bristol apparently did not acquire title to the farm

---

[*]Anna Mary Dunton, *Reflections: Canaan, New York, Bicentennial, 1976* (Canaan, N.Y.: Canaan Historical Society, 1976), p. 2.

until the last day of winter of 1872,[†] when he bought it from his widowed mother for $1.00. Two days later he sold it to William Donnelly for $7,276, accepting a mortgage of $4,376.[‡] Abel then moved to the village of Claverack, spending the remaining eight years of his life there.

Philo Blinn wrote the better part of his diary four miles away, as the crow flies, from where Abel Bristol was farming, and it seems very probable that they were acquainted. I have not found Abel's name in the diary, but Blinn did business with several other members of the Bristol family, including Abel's brother "Scholefield" (Schoville), to whom he traded a large bay horse for a three-year-old mare and $180.[§]

In the early years of the diary, Blinn repeatedly writes of his wish to escape the anxious life of a trader and devote himself only to farming, but trading is where the potential profit was, and as the years advanced Blinn devoted himself increasingly not only to livestock trading but to a variety of other business ventures. The diary also reveals a young Blinn who is acutely conscious of the contest between spiritual and worldly ambition, but with the passage of time the contest becomes less evenly matched, and, progressively, the diarist seems to take his spiritual well-being for granted. This latter Blinn is less interesting to us, but was probably not less interesting to himself.

My understanding of the history of Abel Bristol's barn is surely imperfect, but it would be much more so without the help of my neighbor Martin Andre, and that of Anna Mary Dunton of the Canaan Historical Society, Helen McLeland of the Columbia County Historical Society, and Wendy Fuller of the Chatham Public Library. I am most grateful to the late John Dardess, who transcribed his great-grandfather's diaries and gave a copy of this extraordinary document to the Chatham Public Library; and to his son George Dardess, for his generous encouragement of my project.

J. S.

[†]Columbia County Deed Book 48, p. 414.

[‡]Ibid., p. 416; Columbia County Mortgage Book 28, p. 137.

[§]Blinn diary, vol. 1, p. 85, February 25, 1860; transcript in Chatham Public Library, Chatham, New York.